KU-244-352

Contents

Welcome to Ireland

Are you planning a trip to Ireland? Maybe you are just interested in learning a little about this special country. Perhaps you are the type of person who likes to read about warring Vikings and ancient castles. Whatever your reasons for learning about Ireland, you are sure to be impressed. Ireland is a country with an incredible past, amazing geographical sites, bustling cities and plenty of interesting people.

Tips to get you started

• Use the table of contents

In this book, there may be some sections that interest you more than others. Take a look at the contents page. There, you can pick the chapters that interest you and start with those.

• Use the glossary

When you see **bold** words in the text, you can look them up in the glossary. The glossary will help you learn their meanings. It is found on page 46.

• Use the index

If you need to find information on a very specific topic, turn to the index at the back of the book. The index lists all the subjects covered in the book. It will tell you what pages to find them on.

▲ **DUNGUAIRE CASTLE ON GALWAY BAY**
This beautiful castle was built in 1520. Today, it is open to visitors. There are special medieval banquets every night.

Ireland's past

Before planning a trip to Ireland, find out about Ireland's past. It is filled with incredible stories about everything from knights and battles to widespread hunger and disease. This varied history has played a role in making Ireland what it is today. If you want to understand the places you visit, you will need to read about Ireland's history.

Ancient history

Where did the Irish come from? **Historians** think that people first came to Ireland about 8000 to 9000 years ago. They sailed from Europe and settled in the north of Ireland. The first Irish people survived by hunting and farming. All that remains of their **civilization** today are burial mounds, simple huts and tools.

By 400 BC, another group of Europeans had arrived. They were called the Celts. They took control of most of Ireland. They introduced new farming practices and developed crafts such as pottery and metalworking. Today, Celtic **influence** can still be seen in much of Irish life.

◀ **MEDIEVAL CELTIC ARMOUR**
This Celtic breastplate was made for battle. The Celts came to Ireland in about 400 BC. They were famous for their metalworking.

► VIKING SHIP
The Vikings first came to Ireland in ships like this one. They were great sailors. Viking ships were swift, silent and light. They could easily out-manoeuvre other ships.

Christians and Vikings

In around 400 AD, St Patrick brought the Christian religion to Ireland. He also introduced the Roman alphabet and the Latin language to the Irish. Modern Ireland is still almost entirely Christian and St Patrick is honoured with a special public holiday called St Patrick's Day.

Over the next thousand years, Ireland suffered outbreaks of violence as it came under the control of several different groups of people. Bands of **invaders** called Vikings began arriving by the 700s. Historians tell us that the Vikings liked to hunt. They also fought well using axes and clubs – the men were strong, tough fighters. However, many Vikings eventually settled in Ireland and built towns, including Dublin, Cork and Limerick. They even started farms.

A little later, the Normans conquered Ireland. They came from England and northern France. They were not quite as warlike as the Vikings but were still brave fighters.

▲ 1949, IRISH NATIONALIST DEMONSTRATION
Irish demonstrators show their support for Ireland. In
1949, Ireland won its independence from the British and
became the Republic of Ireland.

The beginning of modern times

The mid–1500s mark the beginning of Ireland's
modern era. It was during this time that England took
control of the island. The English controlled Irish
commerce and, more importantly, they controlled
Irish religion. Irish Catholics fought many battles with
the English Protestants.

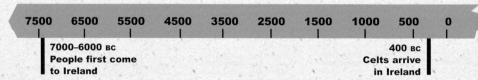

BC 7500 6500 5500 4500 3500 2500 1500 1000 500 0

7000–6000 BC
People first come
to Ireland

400 BC
Celts arrive
in Ireland

In the 1800s, Ireland experienced a terrible tragedy when almost all the potato plants in the country were killed by disease. This caused a **famine** because the Irish depended on potatoes for food. The potato famine lasted from 1845 to 1849. Nearly 1 million people died from starvation and over 1 million more left the country.

Ireland today

In 1949, the Irish declared **independence** and formed the **Republic** of Ireland. The British government agreed to this, but a small section of the northern part of the island remained part of Great Britain. This part is called Northern Ireland.

Today, people are still arguing about Northern Ireland. Some think Northern Ireland should join the Republic of Ireland while others say it should remain part of the United Kingdom. At times, this **dispute** has become violent and many people have died. Everyone is upset by the conflict but no-one is sure how to solve it.

In recent years, the situation has looked more hopeful. World leaders have helped both sides to discuss possible solutions to the problem. There is no easy answer but for now much of the fighting has stopped.

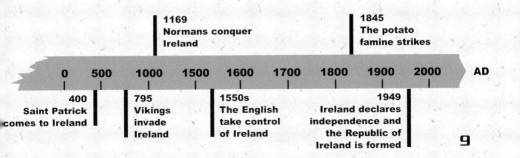

1169
Normans conquer
Ireland

1845
The potato
famine strikes

| 0 | 500 | 1000 | 1500 | 1600 | 1700 | 1800 | 1900 | 2000 | AD |

400
Saint Patrick
comes to Ireland

795
Vikings
invade
Ireland

1550s
The English
take control
of Ireland

1949
Ireland declares
independence and
the Republic of
Ireland is formed

9

A look at Ireland's geography

Ireland is sometimes called the Emerald **Isle** because people think of it as being a deep, brilliant green, like an **emerald**. The island is covered with excellent **pasture-land** which means there is lots of grass and other plants like clover for grazing animals like cows and sheep to eat. The rolling green fields are beautiful to look at. Some people say that the Emerald Isle is the one of the most beautiful places in the world.

Land

Ireland is not just made up of flat pasture land. There are several mountain ranges as well and many of these mountains are near the coast. The main mountain ranges include the Donegal mountains in the north-west, the Wicklow mountains in the east, and the mountains of Connemara in the west.

Ireland's highest peak is in the mountains of Kerry. It is called Carrauntoohill and it stands 1041 metres above sea level.

The mountains surround Ireland's lowlands. These are mostly in the centre of the island. Much of this land was cleared of its natural woodland long ago and it is now used for farms. **Bog** land also makes up much of central Ireland.

FASCINATING FACT

What is a bog? It is wetland made up of decayed plant-life called peat. A peat bog may form over thousands of years where a lake fills up with mud and plants. Peat burns well, so some people use it as a fuel.

▶ IRELAND'S SIZE

The Republic of Ireland covers about 70,280 sq km (27,135 sq miles), about five-sixths of the island of Ireland. The rest of the island is called Northern Ireland, which is part of the United Kingdom. Northern Ireland is 14,147 sq km (5462 sq miles).

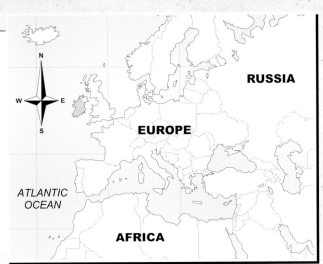

IRELAND

★ National capital

● Major city

— River

| 0 | 25 | 50 Kilometres |
| 0 | 25 | 50 Miles |

Scotland (UK)

Glenveagh National Park

●Donegal

Donegal Bay

Northern Ireland (UK)

Dundalk Bay

●Westport

Fourknocks

Irish Sea

●Athlone

★**Dublin**

●Galway

Galway Bay

ATLANTIC OCEAN

I R E L A N D

●Limerick

Dingle Bay

Kilarney●

Blarney● Cork●

Waterford●

●Wexford

Saint George's Channel

Bantry Bay

Water

To the east of Ireland lie the Irish Sea and St George's Channel. Great Britain lies on the other side of this stretch of water. To the north, south and west is the Atlantic Ocean.

Visitors who want to try fishing should go to the river Shannon, Ireland's longest river. It flows from the north of Ireland south-west to the Atlantic Ocean and it is 370 kilometres (230 miles) long. The Shannon forms several lakes along its course. These include Lough Ree and Lough Derg, also good places for fishing.

A lot of Ireland's shoreline is jagged and rocky. Oceans and rivers have cut deep **bays** into the coastline which provide excellent natural **ports** for boats. Some of the most important ports are Dublin, Cork, Galway and Limerick. Most of Ireland's **foreign trade** passes through these coastal cities.

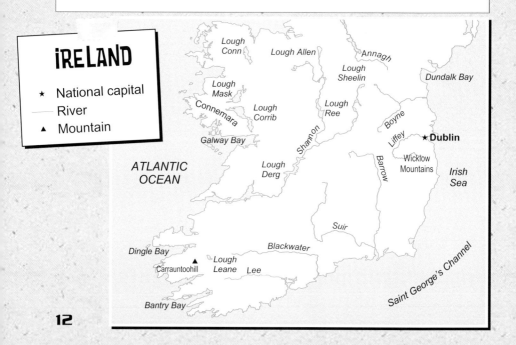

IRELAND

★ National capital
— River
▲ Mountain

Lough Conn
Lough Allen
Annagh
Lough Sheelin
Dundalk Bay
Lough Mask
Connemara
Lough Corrib
Lough Ree
Boyne
Liffey
★ Dublin
Galway Bay
Shannon
Wicklow Mountains
Barrow
Irish Sea
ATLANTIC OCEAN
Lough Derg
Dingle Bay
Blackwater
Suir
Carrauntoohill
Lough Leane
Lee
Saint George's Channel
Bantry Bay

▲ **FISHING ON THE RIVER SHANNON**
The Shannon is Ireland's longest river. This
fisherman enjoys a view of King John's Castle in
Limerick, built in the 1200s.

◀ **SHEEP FARMING**
These farmers are from County Galway, which is a farming area. There are about 600,000 sheep there, making Galway the biggest sheep rearing county in Ireland.

Climate

Ireland has a **temperate** climate. This means that the weather is mild, and does not get very hot or very cold. Temperatures in the winter average about 5°C and in the summer the average temperature is about 15°C.

Ireland is situated as far north as Canada but it does not get as cold. This is because the seas that surround Ireland affect its temperature. In the winter, the Atlantic Ocean and the Irish Sea keep Ireland warm. In the summer, they keep Ireland cool.

The surrounding water has another effect on Ireland – it causes lots of rain. Visitors often complain about the frequent rain, but this is what keeps Ireland green and makes it perfect for farming. Many people say they love Ireland's wet and chilly weather.

Reader's tip: You have just read a lot about the land in Ireland. Can you find the places that are mentioned here on the map on page 12?

▲ **RAINY DAYS**
It can be fun to travel by pony and cart. It rains a lot in Ireland, so be sure to take an umbrella.

Dublin: snapshot of a big city

▲ **DUBLIN**
The river Liffey runs right through the city of Dublin. The Ha'penny Bridge in the foreground is used to cross from one side to the other.

If you like hearing stories about Viking battles, exploring thousand-year-old buildings or wandering through crowds of people in exciting shopping districts Dublin is an ideal place to visit. In Dublin, you can see a **mummified** human heart or browse through hand-painted books from the 12th century. There are places to sit by the river and watch as people pass and beautiful buildings to admire. Dublin has something for every kind of visitor.

City facts

Dublin is Ireland's capital and also its largest city. More than 1 million people live in the Dublin area – that is almost a quarter of the country's population.

Vikings **founded** the city about 1200 years ago. They called the town Dublin, which means 'black pool' in Irish. Experts think there was probably a pool of dark water nearby.

Dublin is Ireland's most important port. Nearly half of the country's foreign trade passes through the city. Goods **imported** from far-off places like Brazil and Greece come through Dublin. Irish goods are often **exported** through this busy port.

Dublin lies at the mouth of the river Liffey, on Ireland's east coast. In fact, the Liffey runs right through Dublin, dividing the city in two. Several beautiful bridges span the river, so it is easy to get around if you are prepared to do a lot of walking.

North of the Liffey

On the north side of the Liffey, the first place to visit is O'Connell Street. It is one of Dublin's best shopping areas and is the perfect place to find some souvenirs to take home. If you like to wander through markets and eat ice cream at pavement cafés, then O'Connell Street should be at the top of your list.

A good way to get to the south side of the river is to walk across the Ha'penny Bridge. It is made of iron and is one of the most popular sights in the city. It was given its nickname because of the toll that used to be charged to cross the bridge – one old half penny.

South of the Liffey

Once you are on the south side of the river, try to visit Trinity College. It is over 400 years old and its **architecture** is some of the most impressive in Ireland.

From there, head south to the National Museum to learn more about Ireland's history and **culture**. Here, you will find **artefacts** and rare objects which will help you learn about Irish history.

Christ Church Cathedral is another good place to visit. It was built at the end of the 12th century and it is full of artefacts, including some from the original Viking settlements. This is where you will find the 800-year-old heart of St Laurence O'Toole, famous for his love of, and **dedication** to, the Irish people. While asking the English king to help his country, he fell sick and died.

► O'CONNELL STREET

O'Connell Street is one of Dublin's most popular spots. It is a great place to sightsee, shop and eat.

DUBLIN'S TOP-TEN CHECKLIST

If you are heading to Dublin, here is a list of the top ten things you should do.

- ☐ Learn more about Irish history at the National Museum.
- ☐ Go to Moore Street Market to look at unusual fish and local cheeses.
- ☐ Visit the old Custom House near the river.
- ☐ Cross the Ha'penny Bridge over the Liffey.
- ☐ Have a picnic on Saint Stephen's Green.
- ☐ People-watch in the Temple Bar area.
- ☐ Go shopping in O'Connell Street.
- ☐ See a play at the famous Abbey Theatre.
- ☐ Wander around the campus of Trinity College.
- ☐ Spend an afternoon at Christ Church Cathedral.

Four top sights in Ireland

There is a lot to learn about Ireland just by looking around. Most people can spend only a limited amount of time on holiday, so it is a good idea to make a plan. Here are a few must-see places:

Blarney Castle

The Irish are known for the 'gift of the gab' – that means they love to talk, and people love to listen. If you are interested in getting the gift of the gab for yourself, visit Blarney Castle, the home of the famous Blarney Stone. **Legend** has it that anyone who kisses this stone will be able to talk like the Irish.

Blarney Castle is in the town of Blarney, in southern Ireland. It is about 8 kilometres (5 miles) from the city of Cork, so it is easy to get to. A local ruler called Cormac Laidhiv McCarthy, the Lord of Muskerry, built the castle in 1446 on the site of a smaller 13th-century castle. It was designed to defend the area from English invaders. Today, a lot of the castle is in ruins because it was attacked by Oliver Cromwell's army in 1646. The keep, or tower house, is still intact. It is here that you will find the Blarney Stone. Blarney Castle is also well known for its beautiful gardens.

The Irish people who built the castle made it very difficult to kiss the Blarney Stone. There are lots of steps to the top of the keep and to kiss the stone you will have to lean backwards over a big drop.

▼ BLARNEY CASTLE

Built in 1446, this castle was designed to keep out invaders. Today, much of it is in ruins – except for the tower that houses the legendary Blarney Stone.

▶ KISSING THE BLARNEY STONE

Legend says that kissing this stone will give you the gift of the gab. It is suspended over the edge of the tower, high off the ground. Someone will help you if you want to kiss the Blarney Stone.

WARNING
BEFORE KISSING THE
STONE REMOVE ALL
LOOSE VALUABLES

Waterford crystal factory

An interesting place to visit is the Waterford glass factory. It was opened by George and William Penrose in 1783. It was in Waterford, on the south-east coast of Ireland. The Penrose brothers chose Waterford because it was a busy port town, which made it easy to ship their products to foreign countries.

The glass made at the Penrose factory is now famous all over the world. It is called crystal. Crystal has a high **lead** content. This means that artists can carve intricate designs into the glass without breaking it. All Waterford crystal is carved by artists who have spent years learning their trade.

The Waterford factory is the largest glass factory in the world. There are daily tours, so it is easy to look round. On the tour, you can watch craftspeople **blow**, cut, shape and carve the crystal. You are allowed to take photographs in many parts of the factory. You can also see a furnace that burns at 1200°C.

Remember that Waterford crystal is very expensive, so be very careful when you visit. You might want to buy some postcards instead, they are much cheaper and less fragile than the real thing.

▶ MOLTEN CRYSTAL

A huge furnace heats ingredients to make molten crystal. Teams of blowers stand by. They use long tubes to blow the crystal into different shapes.

▲ MASTER CUTTERS AT WATERFORD

A master cutter decorates crystal that has already been shaped by a blower. Master cutters are artists. They add a special touch to every pattern they make.

Fourknocks

Few sights in Ireland are as mysterious as this ancient burial **tomb**. Very little is known about the people who built Fourknocks.

Fourknocks is near the village of Naul in County Meath, a district in the middle of Ireland. It is part of a cluster of burial mounds in the area. The most famous of these mounds is the Newgrange Passage Tomb.

The exact age of Fourknocks is still uncertain and is being debated by historians. Some say it could have been built 7000 years ago but others think that it is closer to 4000 years old.

Historians think that the name Fourknocks may come from the ancient Irish words *fuair cnocs*, which means 'cold hills'. It could also refer to the design of the tomb because there are four mounds, or *cnocs*.

Of the four mounds, only one is in good condition. It consists of a long passageway leading to a pear-shaped room which has three small rooms attached to it. When the tomb was first explored, scientists found the remains of several people. The bodies had been burnt to ashes. A few artefacts were also in the chamber. These included a pin made from a deer antler and several rocks carved with a W pattern.

The full story of the people who built Fourknocks has been lost. For the traveller, that is what makes this place so fascinating. The story of these ancient people is still a mystery.

▲ ENTERING AN ANCIENT TOMB
Fourknocks is the site of an ancient burial tomb. Only one out of the four burial mounds is still intact. These visitors are learning the history of this burial ground.

Glenveagh National Park

If you are in the county of Donegal, head to Glenveagh National Park. Glenveagh is the largest park in Ireland and covers about 160 square kilometres (60 square miles). There is plenty for visitors to see – with its mountain ranges and lakes, Glenveagh is one of Ireland's most beautiful regions.

The tallest peak in Glenveagh is Errigal Mountain. It rises 751 metres above sea level. It is one of many beautiful peaks in Glenveagh's Derryveagh range.

Beneath the mountains you will find rolling fields and woodlands. This landscape is home to badgers, foxes, peregrine falcons and the largest herd of red deer in Ireland.

There is a lake in the park called Lough Veagh. On the southern shore sits Glenveagh Castle. This castle was built in 1870 and is open to the public. The surrounding grounds provide views of the lake. It is also popular with photographers.

► GLENVEAGH GARDENS

In 1870, a rich heiress built these gardens behind Glenveagh Castle. The gardens are huge. They display plants and flowers in a rainbow of colours.

▼ ERRIGAL MOUNTAIN

Errigal Mountain is the tallest peak in Donegal. Climbing to the top of Errigal's peak is a favourite activity for visitors.

Going to school in Ireland

Most children attend religious schools in Ireland. Usually they are either Catholic or Protestant. Religious schools are run by churches, but the government helps to pay for them.

On a typical day, children take classes in maths, history and science – just like at school anywhere else. The one unusual subject is Gaelic, or Irish. Gaelic is one of the official languages of Ireland and it comes from ancient language of the Celts.

▲ AN IRISH CLASSROOM
Irish students begin learning Gaelic at an early age. Gaelic has Celtic origins. It is the traditional language of Ireland.

The Irish play all sorts of sports but their favourites are rugby and football. The national rugby and football teams play at the famous Lansdowne Road stadium in Dublin.

The Irish also have sports that no one else plays. The most popular are hurling and Gaelic football. Hurling is similar to field hockey. Gaelic football is a bit like ordinary football, except the players can pick up the ball with their hands.

Visitors who would rather see horses than ball games can go to the races. The Irish love horse racing and hold more than 240 horse-racing events every year.

► **RUGBY PLAYERS**
In rugby, players are allowed to carry, kick and throw the ball. A team scores most points by touching the ball down over the opponents' goal-line, called a try.

From farming to factories

It used to be that most Irish people made a living by farming. Irish soil is very rich and the pasture land is perfect for sheep and cows. Potatoes grow very well in this temperate climate. These days, however, most people work in factories and other businesses. Farming is hard work and it does not always pay very well so fewer and fewer young people are going into farming.

Irish factories make many different things. Ireland's most important products are chemicals, computers, processed foods and medicines. The country is probably most famous for the cut glass, or crystal, made in Waterford. It is also known for the fine wool from the sheep raised on the island.

Like many other countries, Ireland has been changed by the Internet. In recent years, masses of new high-tech companies have moved to the Emerald Isle. The country is now known as the Celtic Tiger because of the success of its new industries. Millions of euros (the currency that has replaced the Irish pound) pour into the marketplace each day. If you want to learn more, look at the quick facts section on pages 42–43.

▲ **PICKING POTATOES**
Ireland is known for its potatoes.

▲ **ON-LINE IN IRELAND**
Students get a lesson in computer use. The Internet
has brought many changes to Ireland. It is now home
to many high-tech companies.

31

The Irish government

Ireland is a **democracy** which means that people vote for members of the government. The head of state is the president. The president has a seven-year term and can serve for two terms. There is also a prime minister, called the Taoiseach in Irish. He or she helps to make and administer Ireland's laws.

Ireland's parliament consists of the House of Representatives and the Senate. The House of Representatives makes the laws. It has 166 members, who each serve for up to five years. The Senate has 60 members. It mostly serves to advise the prime minister and the representatives. That means they tell the rest of parliament what they should do. Sometimes the prime minister and the representatives take their advice, and other times they do not.

IRELAND'S NATIONAL FLAG

The Irish flag is called the Tricolor flag. The green stripe is for the Irish people and their original Green Flag of Ireland. The orange is for the early British colonists. The green also stands for Catholics and the orange for Protestants. The white stripe represents the hope for peace between the two groups.

Religions of Ireland

Ireland is a very religious nation. There is a higher percentage of churchgoers in Ireland than in most other countries in the world.

Nearly 95 per cent of Ireland's population is Roman Catholic. The remaining 5 per cent is mostly Protestant. Over the years, religion has caused conflict between Irish people. In recent times, things have got better. Disputes between different religions have decreased.

One of the best ways to learn about Irish religion is to visit the churches. Some of Ireland's churches are nearly 1500 years old. Visiting some of these buildings will teach you a lot about Ireland and its amazing religious history.

▲ ST PATRICK'S CATHEDRAL
This famous cathedral in Dublin was originally built more than 1500 years ago. St Patrick first brought the Christian religion to Ireland.

Irish food

A lot of Irish food is based on lamb or mutton. Mutton is meat that comes from sheep. It is often served with piping-hot roast potatoes.

Since Ireland produces a lot of dairy foods, there will often be large glasses of milk served. There is often a loaf of brown bread or soda bread and some butter. Soda bread is made using baking soda instead of yeast, and is an Irish speciality.

It is nearly impossible to go to Ireland and not try some of the famous Irish stew. This hot dish is a delicious casserole made from lamb, carrots, potatoes, onions and parsnips. All of this is cooked in one pot. It is perfect for people who have been working outside in the cold all day.

The Irish also make lots of wonderful cakes. One of the most famous Irish cakes is called Barmbrack. The name comes from some Gaelic words which mean 'speckled bread' and it is a light fruit cake flavoured with spices.

◀ IRISH STEW
Irish stew is a perfect meal on a cold, rainy day. It is made with lamb and vegetables such as carrots, onions, parsnips and potatoes.

Irish recipe

IRISH SODA BREAD

INGREDIENTS:
570 g flour
1 tsp baking soda
$\frac{1}{2}$ tsp baking powder
1 tsp salt
120 g butter
1 egg
buttermilk

WARNING:
**Never cook or bake by yourself.
Always ask an adult to help you
in the kitchen.**

DIRECTIONS:
**Ask an adult to help you preheat
the oven to 175° C or gas mark
3–4. Grease a 25-cm round baking
tin and sprinkle it with flour. Sift
together the dry ingredients. Mix
the butter into the dry ingredients with a pastry blender.
Add the raisins. Beat the egg in a measuring jug. Fill
with buttermilk to make 500 ml. Add the egg and
buttermilk mixture to the flour. Mix well with a wooden
spoon. Spread the dough into the well-greased and floured
tin. Bake for 45 minutes. Take out of the pan to cool.
Serve warm with butter.**

Up close: the Celtic Tiger

For a long time, life was very hard in Ireland. The **economy** was in trouble and there were not many good jobs. Now things are changing. There are many new businesses starting in Ireland and the Irish economy is growing. This success means that Ireland is sometimes called the Celtic Tiger.

The Celtic brain-drain

The Internet has affected most of the world and Ireland is no exception. When Ireland's economy was declining, people left Ireland to find good jobs. When the best and most skilled people leave their country to find better jobs, it is called a brain-drain. Ireland has now reversed its brain-drain. Lots of people from other countries are coming to work in Ireland.

The 'cel-tech' revolution

In recent years, lots of high-tech companies have raced to open offices in Ireland. In fact, the Emerald Isle is now being called 'The Silicon Isle'. This name refers to the silicon used to make **microchips**.

▲ **MAKING MICROCHIPS**
Making microchips is a booming industry. In fact,
Ireland is sometimes called 'the Silicon Isle' because
there are so many high-tech companies.

An ultra-modern landscape

So what does all this new economic growth mean to a visitor? First, the landscape is changing rapidly. Huge cranes tower above ancient churches. Brand-new office buildings are squeezed between traditional cottages. Restaurants and shops are busier and more expensive, because there is a lot more money to be spent.

It seems that Ireland is changing, like the rest of the world, and visitors can see plenty of evidence of these changes taking place.

◀ TIMES ARE CHANGING. And so is Ireland's landscape. Modern buildings pop up next to ancient ones. Here, Bunratty Castle in County Clare towers over a shopping district.

▲ **MODERN CITYSCAPE**
Modern Irish cities light up the night. Above, Dublin's skyline is reflected in the river Liffey. With increased economic growth, Ireland's landscape is changing rapidly.

Holidays

Ireland is mostly Christian, so Christmas and Easter are important holidays. St Patrick's Day, on 17 March, is also a religious holiday because St Patrick is the **patron saint** of Ireland. Over the years, St Patrick's Day has also become a celebration of Ireland as a country. All over the world, Irish people celebrate their roots on St Patrick's Day. They have parades and parties and dress up in green.

Another important holiday is Hallowe'en – not just because of the treats, though. Hallowe'en marks the Celtic New Year, and is an ancient festival dating back more than 2000 years.

▲ SAINT PATRICK'S DAY PARADE
The Irish celebrate Saint Patrick's Day with parades. Above, participants are dressed in traditional Celtic clothes. This holiday is a symbol of Irish pride, tradition and heritage.

Learning the language

English	Gaelic	How to say it
Excuse me	Gabh mo leithscéal	GO MO LESH-kul
How are you?	Cén chaio a bhfuil tú	KEH he WIL TU
My name is	(insert name) áta orm	AHtuh OR-uhm
Please	Más è do thoil è	MA-s eh DUH-hil EH
Thank you	Go raibh maith 'ad	go ruh MA-hudh
You're welcome	Tá fáilte romhat	TA FEL-tcha root
Goodnight	Oíche mhaith	EE WAH

Quick facts

Ireland

Capital
Dublin

Borders
Northern Ireland (UK)

Area
70,280 sq km
(27,135 sq miles)

Population
3,883,159

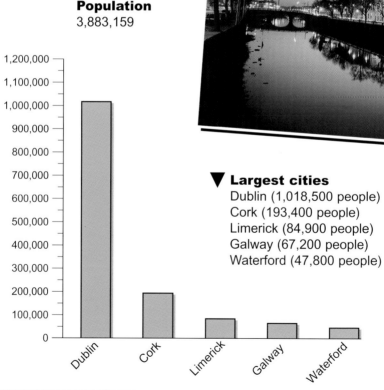

▼ **Largest cities**
Dublin (1,018,500 people)
Cork (193,400 people)
Limerick (84,900 people)
Galway (67,200 people)
Waterford (47,800 people)

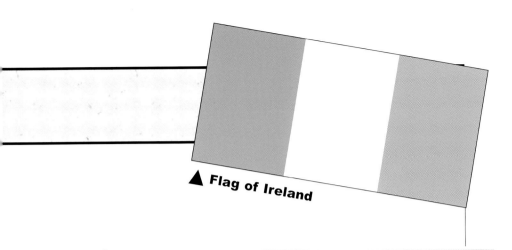

▲ Flag of Ireland

Coastline ▶
1448 km (900 miles)

Longest river
Shannon
370 km (230 miles)

Literacy rate
98% of all Irish people
can read

Major industries
Food products, brewing,
textiles, clothing

**Main crops and
livestock**
Turnips, barley, potatoes,
sugar beet, wheat, cattle

Natural resources
Zinc, lead, natural gas,
barite, copper

◀ **Monetary unit**
Euro

People to know

Many people have helped make Ireland great. Here are some of them.

◄ William Butler Yeats

William Butler Yeats was born in Dublin in 1865. He first became known for his poems about Irish myths and history. Later in life, he wrote about events in his own time. These poems made him famous throughout the world.

► Mary Robinson

In 1990, Mary Robinson became the seventh president of Ireland. She was born in County Mayo, where she studied to be a lawyer. Robinson ended her term as president in 1997. She then went on to work for the United Nations.

◄ Enya

If you've heard Enya sing, then you've heard the Irish language. Enya records many of her songs in Irish. She has sold more than 60 million albums. Her music has been used for many films, including *Lord of the Rings*.

More to read

Do you want to know more about Ireland?
Take a look at the books below.

See Through History: The Celts, Hazel Mary Martell
(Heinemann Library, 1995)
Discover life in the land of the Celts and see inside
Celtic buildings including a house, a tomb, a stone tower
and a monastery.

Turning Points in History: Irish Famine, Tony Allan
(Heinemann Library, 2001)
Find out about the events that led up to the famine in
Ireland and the effect this had on the country.

Beliefs and Myths of Viking Britain, Martin Whitlock
(Heinemann Library, 1997)
Learn what the Vikings believed and what every day
religious life was really like for the Vikings in Britain.

Glossary

architecture style or design used in a building
artefact object that was made by humans in the past
bay area of the ocean that is partly closed off by land
blow in glass-blowing, to blow air into a piece of
molten glass, ready for shaping
bog spongy, wet area of land
civilization society with a high state of cultural,
political, social and intellectual development
climate typical weather in a place
commerce the way goods are bought and sold
culture way of life and values of a particular society or
civilization
dedication act of giving giving all one's interest and
work to a particular cause or belief
democracy form of government in which the people
vote for their government officials
dispute disagreement
economy country's way of running its industry, trade
and finances
emerald green gemstone
export to send something out of a country for sale
famine significant or dangerous lack of food
foreign trade the buying or selling of goods from
another country
found to start or set-up something
historian someone who studies the past
independence state of being self-governing and not
under the control of another country

influence effect of a person or thing on another

invader person who enters another country by force

import bring items into a country from another place for sale

isle small island

lead type of metal that is soft and grey in colour

legend old story passed down through the generations; legends can be made-up stories

microchip electrical circuit printed on a small piece of silicon to be used in a computer or electronic equipment

mummified refers to a dead body that has been preserved using special salts and resins and then wrapped in cloth

pasture-land large grassy area that can be used by grazing animals

patron saint saint regarded as the protector of a certain group or nation

port city where ships can safely dock to load and unload cargo

republic form of government, without a monarch, in which the people vote for their government officials

temperate area with a climate of moderate temperatures

tomb room or building made to house a dead body

Index